Drying and Preserving Flowers

Drying and Preserving Flowers

Winifrede Morrison

B T Batsford Limited

To my husband
with love

© Winifrede Morrison 1973
First published 1973
ISBN 0 7134 2324 2

Filmset by Servis Filmsetting Limited Manchester
Printed and bound in Great Britain by
William Clowes Limited Beccles Suffolk
for the publishers
B T Batsford Limited
4 Fitzhardinge Street, London W1H 0AH

Acknowledgment

I would like to thank my husband for his help with checking and typing the manuscript and for some photography. I also thank Mrs J Middleditch for permission to include her dried flower picture on plate 3, and Frank Martin for taking the majority of the black and white photographs.

Buckinghamshire 1973   WDM

Contents

Introduction

Here are some ideas for the times when fresh flowers are not readily available.

Details of design are not given as it is assumed that the arranger who turns to this branch of flower arranging already has some knowledge of the art in general.

It is in January and February that the catalogues arrive and seeds must be ordered. If a heated glasshouse is available, some seeds may be sown at this time. It is a good time too to prepare containers for use later on. Garden work starts in March, and of course the first few months of the year are useful for those long dark evenings which leave more leisure to make pressed flower pictures. January, February and March provide spring flowers for drying in silica gel, borax or sand; and from April onwards there is always some plant material to pick for drying, preserving or pressing. From October to November fresh flowers are scarce and expensive, so then is the time to create something beautiful with the material collected during summer, and to make pot-pourri. These arrangements last a long time and can be put carefully away when fresh flowers come round again. They are invaluable for homes with central heating and for busy people who enjoy natural plant material in preference to plastic. December is, of course, the time to start on ideas for Christmas.

Differing climates mean only different timing. The ideas and sequence remain the same, and move from hot to cold and *vice versa*.

There are many different ways of drying and preserving fresh plant material. By material, I mean flowers, foliage, grasses and almost anything that grows. The method adopted will possibly depend on the time and space available. For instance, drying in silica gel or borax needs space to store large boxes and is far from foolproof! But the result, when successful, is delightful and full of colour. Air drying requires a fairly large number of hooks, or a line in a dry area; and glycerine needs space for a collection of jars, carefully stored upright. Skeletonising is messy, but pressed flowers for pictures need only a small press and a large book – one of the heavier telephone directories for instance.

Many people – and I have been among them – look on dried arrangements as dull and dusty. But, while writing this book, I have tried out everything mentioned in it, and have been truly surprised by the unusual and delightful results obtained.

1 Massed triangle in Oriental figurine
Grasses, *Limonium* (sea lavender), *Cineraria* leaf (pressed) and skeleton *Magnolia* leaves
Arrangement in shades of violet and grey. Figure is grey, base is of violet velvet

Air drying

Air drying is the easiest and most commonly used method. It does not require special preparation and consists simply of hanging up the chosen material to dry.

A general rule on the right time to pick material is to watch for the moment of full maturity, since it is not possible to name an exact time for anything. Seasons vary enormously, and what may work one year may not do so the next; so some degree of trial and error is inevitable. If the material is at the seedhead stage, then this must be ripe, but not over-ripe.

Pick the chosen material and strip the leaves from the stems. They shrivel anyway and are useless, so it is easier to take them off while they are moist. Keep the picked material in small bunches of one kind if possible, and tie each bunch fairly tightly with string, leaving a small loop to hang on the nail or line. The bunches may have to be re-tied as they dry, since the stems shrivel and can slip out of the tie. Plastic ties are even better than string because they can be tightened more easily.

The bunches must be hung, each on a separate hook, on wire coat-hangers or well apart on a line (figure 2). The place in which they hang is important – it must not be damp or too hot, and should be as dark as possible. This helps the material to dry quickly and improves the final

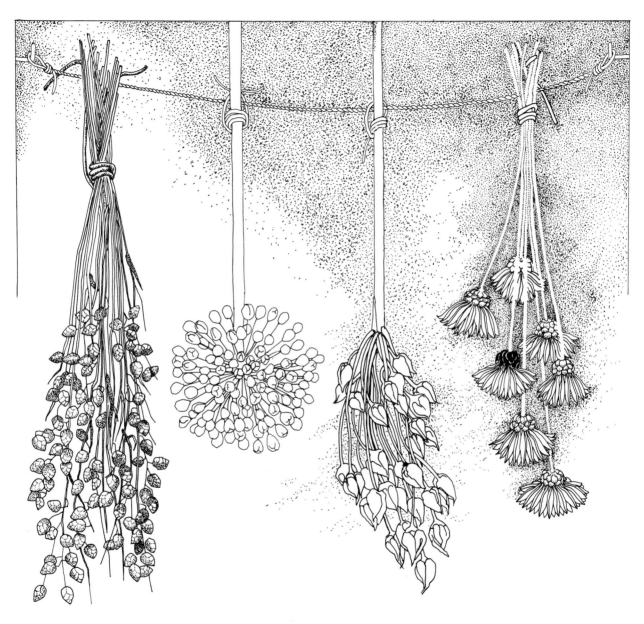

2 Air drying

colouring. It is necessary to have air circulating around the drying plant material; specially large or delicate heads can be stored upright in bottles or jars. Another advantage of this latter method is that the stems tend to settle with a slight curve, and are not as stiff and straight as those which have been dried by hanging. But make sure that anything done this way already has a good firm stem; if the flower or seedhead has any tendency to droop at the neck, remove it to the hanging department. If a curve is required, insert a stub wire into the stem before drying.

The amount of time necessary for complete drying varies according to the material used, the time at which it is picked, the temperature – and even the atmosphere. Fragile material and grasses do not take much longer than a week, but larger moist flowers may need at least three weeks. Very special bits could be dried in a cool airing cupboard but would need careful watching. If the area for drying is not as clean and dry as required, some of the material can be put in to large plastic bags; but make sure these have plenty of air-holes. When the whole stem and head feel quite dry and de-hydrated, the material is ready for storage. Sometimes the stem will shrivel completely (this happens with most of the everlasting flowers), and it is best then to remove most of it before drying and to insert a stub wire (figure 3). This can be covered later with another false stem, florist's tape or a drinking straw.

An understanding of the structure of flowers and seed-heads is a great help in successful preservation, and the book to which I turn when in doubt is *Botany for Flower Arrangers* by John Tampion and Joan Reynolds, published in Great Britain by Pelham Books and in the United States by Drake Publishers; it explains the whys and wherefores very clearly.

I have grouped some of the material suitable for air drying under the heading of the shapes they offer and I have added notes which seem relevant. Most of the Latin

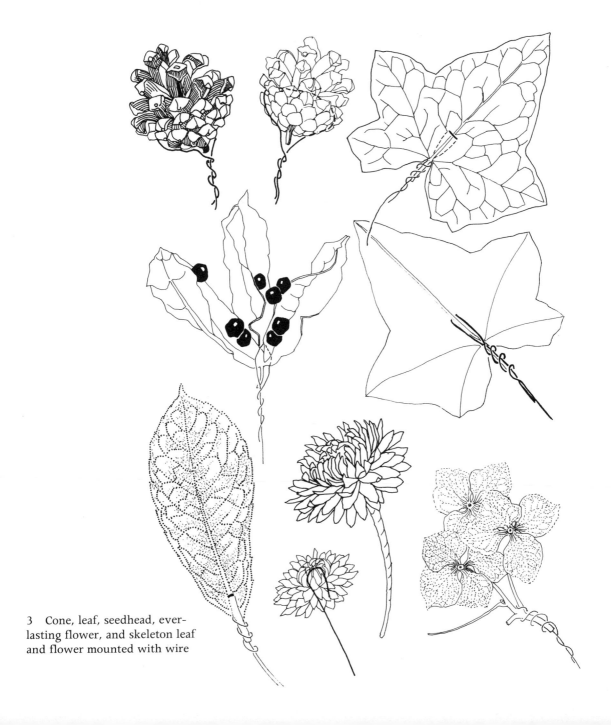

3   Cone, leaf, seedhead, everlasting flower, and skeleton leaf
and flower mounted with wire

13

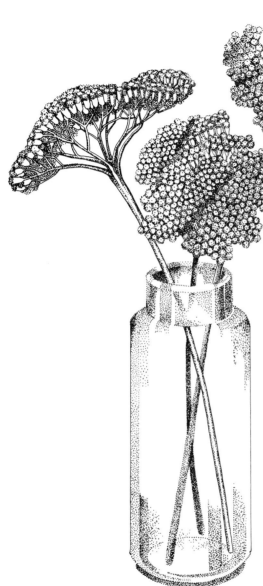

names are taken from *The Dictionary of Garden Plants* by Roy Hay and Patrick M. Synge, published in collaboration with the Royal Horticultural Society by Ebury Press and Michael Joseph. Of course, this list is not complete and most people will wish to add their own favourites. I am all for trying absolutely any kind of plant material; for, after all, what is there to lose? It would otherwise go on the compost heap or in the rubbish bin. Sometimes surprising and rewarding results are obtained.

Note
A very small amount of plant material has to be preserved by first placing the stems in water before drying. As this group includes *Moluccella* and *Hydrangea,* it cannot be omitted.

Cut the *Hydrangea* on the new stem if possible; the *Moluccella* must not be gathered until the tiny flower in the top bract is open (the delightful green bells are really bracts, not flowers). Be sure to remove all the leaves. Now stand the stems in about 50 mm (2 in.) of water in a warm room. When the water has disappeared, hang the stems in bunches and air dry as for the other material. *Hosta* leaves and seedheads can also be dried by this method.

4 Air drying large or delicate heads, showing slight curve in the stems

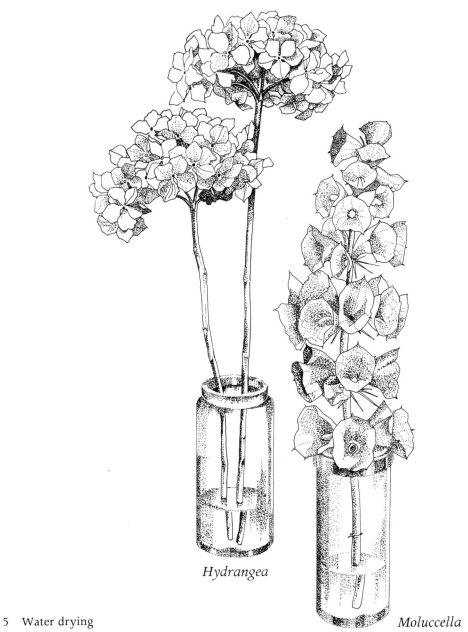

Hydrangea

Moluccella

5   Water drying

Material suitable for air drying

P = perennial HA = hardy annual HHA = half-hardy
annual SH = shrub T = tree.

1   ROUNDED SHAPES

Achillea millefolium (wild yarrow) P
Found in the lanes and hedges; usually white but some-
times a delicate pale pink
Achillea filipendulina (garden yarrow) P
Gather this when mature; it is one of the sure successes for
drying. Dry by standing upright in an empty jar; large
flower heads will not then be damaged
Astrantia maxima (masterwort) P
Delicate little flowers, pinkish green. Dry to a soft brown.
Although brittle, they look very charming in a small
arrangement
Catananche coerulea (Cupid's dart) P
Almost an everlasting; very dainty blue or white
EVERLASTINGS
Ammobium alatum (winged everlasting) HHA
Silvery white bract with yellow centre
Anaphalis (pearl everlasting) P
Soft grey leaf and white flower
Helichrysum bracteatum (straw flower) HHA
The toughest of the everlastings and extremely useful to
give depth and colour. Must be cut when mature but before
the true flowers in the centre are fully open. The bright
papery surround is really a bract. Try to include a few
smaller flowers or buds to give variety. The stems will
shrivel and need stub wires before or after drying

PLATE 1

Cone arrangement with poppy seedheads,
Helichrysums, cones and beech nuts

Large arrangement with dyed pampas and cycas,
Eucalyptus, teazles, cardoon and imported wood lily

2 SPIKY SHAPES

Acanthus spinosus (bear's breeches) P
Very useful for pedestals and large arrangements. Do not pick for drying until the top flower on the spike is open
Aruncus sylvester (goat's beard) (formerly *Spiraea*) P
The fluffy white or pink heads will dry to a soft pretty brown
Celosia argentea plumosa (cockscomb) HHA
Hardly distinguishable from fresh, if gathered at the right time: mature, but not over-ripe
Delphinium P
To preserve the colour, pick immediately the top floret opens and hang upside down. Can still give interesting seedhead if allowed to dry on the plant
Delphinium (larkspur) HA
Dries best if left in small amount of water
Limonium sinuatum (sea lavender) HHA
Fairly strong colours, pinks and purples
Limonium suworowii (statice) HHA
Rose pink spikes; must be mature when cut
Solidago (golden rod) P
A good variety is *goldenmosa,* which has daintier seed-heads than some other varieties

3 LEAVES

Aspidistra (parlour palm) P
Will dry with a curved leaf
Aucuba japonica (spotted laurel) SH
Smooth texture
Grevillea rosmarinifolia SH
Long spiky leaves, usually obtainable from the florist
Stachys lanata (lamb's tongues) P
A soft grey leaf, often more attractive if used back to front

17

4 CLUSTERS OR SPRAYS

Acacia dealbata (mimosa) T
This loses all its fluff, but the tiny yellow balls are most attractive, and keep some of their perfume
Alchemilla mollis (ladies' mantle) P
Dries a soft yellowish green with delicate sprays
Amaranthus caudatus (love lies bleeding) HA
The green variety will dry a better colour if kept in darkness
Eryngium (sea holly) P
Be careful not to allow this to become too mature or the seedheads will drop.
Gypsophila elegans (baby's breath) HA or P
Ethereal

5 GRASSES

Briza maxima or *minor* (pearl grass) HA
Dry these, as all grasses, in a cool dry place, certainly not too hot
Cortaderia (pampas grass) P
These stately feathery plumes are not to be despised, in spite of their Victorian associations! They are good in large arrangements and, taken apart, can be used in something quite small
Festuca ovina (glauca) (sheep's fescue) P
Good bluish-grey colour
Lagurus ovatus (hare's tail) HA
Very soft fluffy grass
Phalaris arundinacea ('Picta' ribbon grass) P
White stripes on narrow green leaves
Stipa calamagrostis or *pennata* (feather grass) P
Long stems with feathered heads

These are only a few of the many available grasses. Any kind of corn (wheat or barley) is very useful and it is a good idea to sow a handful of chicken corn in a spare corner of ground.

6 SEEDHEADS

A = annual   B = biennial   BB = bulb   C = corm

Aconitum (monkshood) P
There are several varieties of blue *Aconitums* which leave good seedheads on a long spiky stem. There is also a yellow variety (*Lycoctonum*) but I have not tried this

Alliums (onion family) P
So many varieties, large and small, but they all make delightful seedheads (even if they smell like onions). They need to be dried upside down if possible, because of their rather fleshy stems, but with the round heads well protected from damage

Angelica officinalis (Holy Ghost) P
Use the stem for candying, then hang head upside down, as above

Aquilegia (columbine) P
Delicate seedheads

Clematis (virgin's bower) P
Most of the clematis form fascinating seedheads, rather like large spiders, especially the wild one

Clematis vitalba (old man's beard)
They must be watched so that they do not get too fluffy; a few squirts of colourless hair lacquer will help to prevent this

Crocosmia crocomiiflora (montbretia) C
Both seedheads and leaves will dry well

Cynara cardunculas (cardoon) P
Leaves do not dry, but the seedhead is magnificent. Cut at various stages

Cynara scolymus (globe artichoke) P
As for Cardunculas

Delphinium P
Hollow stems, so must be dried upside down. If they have been allowed to finish flowering and have not been picked to preserve the colour, the seedheads will be interesting

Delphinium (larkspur) A

A finer type of seedhead

Digitalis (foxglove) HA

I allow mine to get very dry in the garden; remove the leaves and hang

Dipsacus fullonium (teasels) P

May be left in the wild until almost ready. Very useful for large arrangements

Epilobium (willow herb) P

Another tall spike, useful for large arrangements. If the seedheads turn fluffy, they will need spraying with hair lacquer

Hosta (plantain lily)

Iris B

Many iris have gorgeous seedheads. Among the best – *Foetidissima* with bright orange berries (which need fixing with hair lacquer)

Lilliums (lily) BB

The martagons have very good seedheads

Lunaria (honesty) HB

I consider this gives very good value. Deep purple flowers early in the year, then lovely flat silvery seedheads which can be used dry or edged with glitter for Christmas. When the outside pod is taken off, the seeds can be used for another crop.

Macleaya formerly *Bocconia, cordata* or *microcarpa* (plume poppy) P

Leave to dry on the plant

Nigella (love-in-a-mist) HA

The foliage must be taken off but the seedhead is charming and often a soft purplish tone. Pretty if painted then glittered on the top

Papaver (poppy) (various) A or B

Again no foliage but very good seedheads. May be treated in the same way as *Nigella* for Christmas

Rumex (dock or sorrel) P
Attractive spiky stems
Tulipa (tulip) B
Not good for the bulb, but if left to go to seed, make fine seedheads
Verbascum (mullein) P or B
Wild and cultivated; nice long spikes

7 FRUITS, ETC

Cones (fir, cedar, larch, etc) will close up in damp conditions but can be opened by drying in a cool oven
Cucurbita (gourds) HHA
Must be allowed to ripen and treated carefully so that they do not get damaged. Bore a hole for a stick or stub wire, then cover all over with clear varnish, especially the hole
Nicandra physaloides (shoofly plant) HA
An unusual shape. The seedhead inside the calyx may be glittered at Christmas.
Physalis franchetii (Chinese lantern or Cape gooseberry) P
Gives a touch of colour as the calyx is bright orange
Zea Mays (maize or Indian corn) HA
The American coloured varieties produce attractive purple heads, but the ordinary one is good, too. Do not take off the papery leaves around the corn-head – they can be opened out to look very decorative. The cob must be mature and will almost certainly need mounting on a strong false stem
Araucaria (monkey puzzle tree) T
Pieces from this tree provide dramatic shape and texture
Vegetable seedheads Carrot, parsnip, leek.

Other drying

Another method of preserving flowers is by using powdered borax, silica gel, sand, or one of the proprietary mixtures now available. Foliage does not take so kindly to it; but the result with flowers preserved in this way is enchanting. They keep their colour and their shape; it is possible, indeed, to use daffodils in September to great effect.

The flowers must be perfectly dry and well-conditioned before inserting in the mixture, and, as the stems will be brittle when ready for use, it may be best to insert a false stem before drying. Personally, I do not do this as I find that the wire stems make things difficult when drying the flower heads. It is possible to put the false stems on afterwards with a very gentle touch.

Which to use is a matter of personal preference. I have used borax and silica gel, also the special mixture, but I cannot speak from experience about sand, though I have seen some very good results by this method.

I use a large square biscuit tin and cover the base with borax, carefully smoothing out any lumps. I then make a shelf of 15 mm ($\frac{1}{2}$ in.) mesh wire half-way down the tin. By cutting the sheet of wire a little larger than the size of the tin the edge can be folded underneath to support the shelf. The flowers, with very short stems, are then inserted head uppermost between the mesh, each one separate from

6   Drying in silica gel, powdered
borax or sand
Flowers supported by 15 mm
($\frac{1}{2}$ in.) mesh wire, and covered
with powder

the next; powdered borax is then sprinkled over them. Be certain that the powder goes into the centre of the flower head and between the petals, also that every flower is covered all round and on top. Make sure, too, that the petals are not bent or distorted in any way. Put the tin away somewhere warm and well out of any damp; damp is fatal to successful drying. This method also applies to the other preserving mixtures.

Various flowers take various times and it is necessary to experiment until the best results are obtained. I do this by gently scraping away the powder over one of the flowers to see if the petals feel strong and slightly papery – which means they are ready to come out. If there is the slightest suspicion of moisture, re-cover the flower and leave a little longer. Certainly, the minimum is about two days for most things; often much longer. Silica gel is usually quicker than borax, but I find it rather too heavy for delicate flowers.

Remove the flowers gently when they feel dry and firm; then store in a dark place, preferably a covered box, with a few crystals of silica gel to ward off any moisture. Both the crystals and the powders may be used over and over again.

Flowers with false stems, in powder

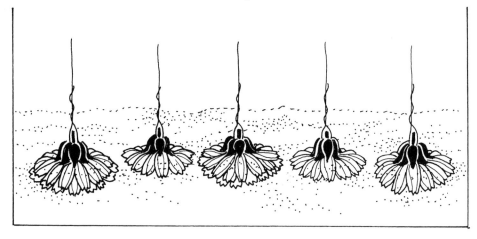

Flowers suitable for preserving by these methods

Zinnias
Most of the daisies and open-faced flowers, for instance, anemones, scabious, marigolds and cornflowers
Nigella (love-in-a-mist).

I have had great success with most of the *Hellebores* except *niger*; and, on the whole, I do not recommend trying any pure white flowers by this method. The green *Hellebore* (*viridis*) and the purple one (*orientalis*) produce excellent dried flowers by the borax method. Condition them well first, by putting the stem ends in boiling water or above a flame for a few seconds before steeping them in water.

Some of the stemmed flowers such as *Delphinium* and larkspur will give good results, but are a little difficult to immerse in the powder; nothing too frail or delicate should be attempted. Small roses – *Carole* or similar – are good, but be sure to get the powder between the petals. Large roses are not often successful.

Preserving in glycerine

This method replaces the water in the plant material with glycerine, thus making it supple and almost everlasting.

The material to be preserved must be gathered before the sap starts to leave the stems, and it should then be conditioned by standing it in deep water for some hours before starting the glycerine treatment. All damaged or eaten leaves must be removed; they take up precious fluid which can be used elsewhere. The branches should not be too long, otherwise they may wither at the tip before the glycerine reaches it; and all the leaves must be washed if at all dirty. If the stems are woody, they can be split to make sure the fluid penetrates and that there is no air lock.

There are various schools of thought on the proportion of glycerine to water, but I use one part of each with good results. Some people recommend one part glycerine and two parts hot water; sometimes ordinary car anti-freeze will work – but not always! In theory, the mixture replaces the water in the stems, therefore it follows that these stems must be full of sap when gathered. If this is receding – a guide to this is the colour when the Autumn tints are showing – it is too late to preserve them in glycerine. But do not lose heart; other methods may be used. The glycerine mixture must penetrate the stem before the barrier known as *abscission* is formed.

Put the stems in about 100 mm (4 in.) of solution, wedge them firmly in position and leave for about two to three weeks. The time varies according to the condition and type of leaves, but can be judged by feeling their suppleness and watching the change of colour. Do not allow the solution to start dripping off the end of the leaves. Remove them immediately they have changed colour completely. If the leaves seem to flag after they have been taken out of the mixture, hang them upside down for a few days so that the glycerine gets right to the top.

Some small leaves, such as *Hedera* (ivy), lily-of-the-valley, etc, can be completely submerged, and the general process of preservation can be speeded with tough leaves – such as *Aucuba* (spotted laurel) and *Aspidistra* – by coating the leaves with some of the solution before the stems are immersed. Make sure that the branch is pruned, hammered and conditioned before starting glycerine treatment.

Some very beautiful and subtle colours result from this method, ranging from a dark leathery brown to soft cream or dark red – and they never look dull or dead. Put them away at the end of the winter and they will come out again next year as good as new. Once the mixture is prepared, it can be used and added to, over and over again; and endless experiments can be tried, with interesting results.

One of the most beautiful things to preserve in glycerine is the bract of *Moluccella laevis* (bells of Ireland) which produces a curved stem in a soft cream colour; but, on the whole, this method is best applied to foliage. If the same kind of material is put into the solution at differing times, a good variation of colour will result.

Flowers suitable for glycerine treatment

Moluccella laevis (bells of Ireland). Make sure that the topmost flower is out before cutting these (the bells are really bracts). I usually cut off the first one or two flowers at the tip as often the glycerine will not penetrate as far as this. They also need to be kept in a fairly dry place while the mixture is working, as they become mouldy very quickly.
Hydrangea
Polygonatum multiflorum (Solomon's seal)
Clematis vitalba (old man's beard – wild clematis). Sometimes the flower heads fix into a delightful soft spidery brown cluster; but, even if they eventually go fluffy, they do not disintegrate. The leaves, too, turn a deep bronze
Digitalis (foxglove). Make sure the top flower is open, though only the seedheads will preserve
Tilia (lime). Remove leaves

Leaves suitable for glycerine treatment

Aspidistra lurida (parlour palm). This will take a very long time, anything up to six months, but is well worth while. It can be hastened by wiping the leaves with glycerine first

7   *Garrya elliptica* preserved by
glycerine method

Aucuba (spotted laurel)
Castanea sativa (sweet chestnut)
Choisya ternata (Mexican orange)
Convallaria majalis (lily-of-the-valley)
Elaeagnus. Also very slow
Eucalyptus (gum). As *Eucalyptus*, especially gunnii, can be cut back, the prunings may be kept for drying or preserving
Fagus sylvatica (beech). It is essential to pick this while the leaves are still green (though not too young) and without any hint of yellow colouring. It is necessary to prune it well and to cut away leaves eaten by insects. The tiny nuts will glycerine, too, if left on the branch
Fatsia japonica
Grevillea robusta (silk bark oak). Fern-like leaf sprays
Grevillea rosmarinfolia. Spiky leaves
Hedera (ivy). Leaves need to be immersed in solution. Berries sometimes do well, too
Helleborus (Christmas rose, Lenten rose, etc)
Laurus nobilis (bay). Rather slow
Magnolia grandiflora
Mahonia japonica
Pittosporum tenuifolium. Cut or buy before too mature as it drops easily
Paeonia (peony)
Quercus (oak). Very pretty if the acorns are included. The corns may drop out but the little cups will remain
Rhododendron
Sorbus aria (whitebeam)
Viburnam tinus (laurestinus)

Overleaf
9 *Top* citrus 'flower' and skeleton *Magnolia*
Right *Garrya elliptica* and *Galpheria*
Centre citrus 'flowers'
Left *Mahonia*

10 Glycerined *Grevillea robusta* and *Aspidistra,* dried martagon lily, skeleton *Hydrangea,* dried citrus skins and *Helichrysums*

8 Glycerined *Moluccella* (bells of ▶ Ireland) with dried cardoon seedheads, honesty, *Delphinium* seedheads, *Astrantia* and *Papaver* (poppy)

PLATE 2

Arrangement in wooden box
Glycerined *Hellebore* leaf and holly, *Grevillea*,
skimmea, *Aspidistra, Garrya elliptica* and
Galpheria leaf

Glycerined *Moluccella* and beech in brass candlestick

11　Material preserved in
glycerine and some skeleton
Magnolia leaves

12　Corsages made with dried,
glycerined and preserved flowers,
leaves and seedheads all wired
and mounted

Pressing for arrangements

This is a useful method because it means that some of the vivid colours of autumn can be caught in all their glory. It is also convenient to be able to do some of the things which should have been done earlier, but may have been missed or forgotten.

It applies mostly to material which has a habit of flat growth, and to single leaves, ferns, grasses and bracken – though it is possible to press sprays of foliage too.

Make sure the material is dry and clean. Do not gather it when wet, if avoidable. It can be carefully cleaned after picking by the use of a slightly dampened tissue. Place it between sheets of newspaper, as flat as possible, and try not to let it overlap. If this cannot be avoided, place a small piece of paper (again, tissues are ideal) between the over-lapping leaves. Then put it underneath a carpet or under heavy weights. Special leaves may be put between sheets of waxed paper, then into the newspaper, before pressing with a cool iron. The wax will melt onto the leaves and form a thin coating.

The time taken before it is ready for use will depend on the temperature, but it is usually about three weeks. This kind of material will always be brittle and needs rather careful handling. If it curls again when dry, the cool iron treatment will flatten it out well. It is also a good idea to be gentle with the carpet sweeper if the leaves are under the carpet! Try if possible to use a bedroom carpet where there is not quite so much traffic.

Most of the leaves will require a false stem of stub wire added when the leaves are pliable; but as this is sometimes difficult, make a small hole in the leaf before pressing and insert a stub wire later. It can be attached with sticky tape quite successfully. Some people submerge the material in a weak starch mixture before pressing; this does add firmness, but it takes time and is a bit messy.

Material suitable for drying and pressing

Acers (sycamore, maple)
Adiantum (maidenhair fern)
Aspidistra lurida (parlour palm)
Athyrium felix-femina (lady fern)
Caladium candidum
Croscosimia (montbretia) .
Gladioli leaves
Hosta formerly *Funkia* (plantain lily)
Osmunda (fern)
Phormium tenax (New Zealand flax)
Vitis (vine). Various

Many leaves of various greenhouse plants, and some from the hedges – blackberry, for instance.

Skeletonising

Many leaves can be found already skeletonised, but it takes time and an eagle eye to discover them. They will probably be underneath trees, half-buried beneath rotting vegetation. Force a way into an old prickly holly tree (wearing gloves and a thick old coat!) and the reward will be great. Rhododendrons, laurel and camellia are good sources of supply, too. Skeletonised *Magnolia* leaves can be bought from florists, usually around Christmas time; they add an ethereal touch to an arrangement.

To skeletonise these at home, collect well-shaped leaves which are not damaged, and which have not started to curl or dry. Remove them from the main stem and, if there is no hurry, simply leave them outside, steeped in rainwater; this may be topped up but must not be cleaned or changed. This process takes a long time and is a bit smelly. After six to eight weeks, they should be slippery and the green surface will feel soft. Pull the surface gently away and wash the leaves – very gently. If they are not white enough, steep them in a gentle solution of household bleach for a few hours, then wash again before drying between soft paper under a weight (except for holly leaves which curl naturally).

A quicker way to achieve a skeleton leaf is to put a handful of soda in a pan of water (preferably rainwater). Do not use an aluminium pan as the soda will render it unfit for any other use. Boil the leaves in this mixture for about an hour — the time is rather a matter of trial and error as some leaves take longer than others.

Take one out occasionally and put it in cool water, or under a running tap, and try it to see if the soft part comes away easily. It is best to wear rubber gloves for this job. Again, these leaves can be whitened by immersing in weak bleach before a final rinse, and then dried. If these leaves seem rather flat when finished, they can be curled to order by wrapping around a small stick or pencil.

I have also skeletonised *Hydrangea* heads most successfully and they are extremely beautiful. I picked some old *Hydrangea* bracts which had been left on the bush throughout the winter and pulled them apart into small clusters. I steeped these in a very strong solution of household bleach, about six parts bleach to one of water for an hour or so. (Wear rubber gloves!) It was fascinating to watch the gradual emergence of the veins. Then I rinsed and dried them on blotting paper, very gently. They were brittle but so delicate. I have used them in a swag with most satisfactory results.

The bracts of *Moluccella* can also be skeletonised as well as the balloon-like heads of *Nicandra*.

The finished material

Unfortunately, it is true that dried and preserved arrangements have a reputation in some quarters for being dull and dreary, but this is not necessarily so. Of course, there are no really vivid colours, but there is a subtlety and beauty in a well-designed dried arrangement which often demands a closer examination. Thought must be given to the contrast of texture and shape of material and to the container to be used. The arrangements must never be allowed to get dusty, and I find it a good idea to remove a dried arrangement occasionally – for instance, if I have some fresh flowers – and then to replace it. I look at it with a fresh eye and start to enjoy it all over again. At the end of the winter, the arrangement is dismantled and the material stored away for use another year, when it will probably be arranged in a different container and a different shape.

Much of the plant material will need false stems before use, and florist's stub wires are necessary for this. A general guide to these wires is the lower the gauge number, the thicker the wire. For instance, the finest reel or rose wire (and electrical fuse wire can be substituted for this) is 34 and 32 gauge; and this is necessary for delicate leaves such as *Magnolia*, and for attaching work on swags. Gauges 20, 22, and 24 are the most useful ones for leaves and for many flowers, such as *Helichrysums*; thicker wires may be used for mounting cones. Sometimes the wire can be covered with florist's tape (it is possible to obtain this in a soft brown) or hidden with another false stem. The hollow stalks of corn are ideal for this. Many of the soft seedheads can be persuaded to last longer by spraying with colourless hair lacquer, which is also useful for prolonging the life of berries.

False flowers, too, can be made very easily and are extremely effective. Take the moon-shaped pods of honesty (*Lunaria*) and mount five of them on fine reel wire. Group them around a small poppyhead or a tiny cone for a centre, and wire the whole group firmly together, taking the wires down to form a stem which can then be covered as suggested above. Various combinations of leaves can be used this way and very large 'flowers' made for massive arrangements. I have used *Eucalyptus* leaves around the seedhead of *Santolina* to make a sort of flat cabbage rose type of flower; and I have also grouped several layers of skeleton *Magnolia* around a bleached poppyhead, with great effect.

The mechanics of arranging are only slightly different from those used for fresh flowers; and of course the principles of design are the same. Sometimes crumpled 50 mm (2 in.) mesh wire netting alone may not be secure enough for fine wire stems, and there are various alternatives. One is *Plasticine*. A large lump of this, preferably brown or fawn in colour, should be firmly fixed to the base of the chosen container (usually a shallow one is best for this method). The container must be very dry, and it is necessary to make sure there is no air lock between the base of the bowl and the *Plasticine*. Press it down firmly all round and try to lift the container by the *Plasticine* alone to make sure it is secure. Then, of course, arranging is easy as the stems can be manoeuvred in any direction and changed at will. If the arrangement is to be more or less permanent, a mixture of plaster filling or powdered deter-

Honesty seedpods wired
individually, then grouped
together with centre seedhead

Three *Eucalyptus* leaves held by
wired seedhead centre

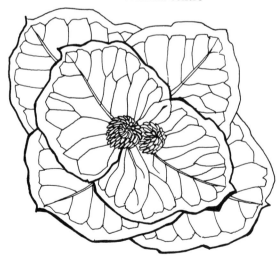

13   Making a false flower

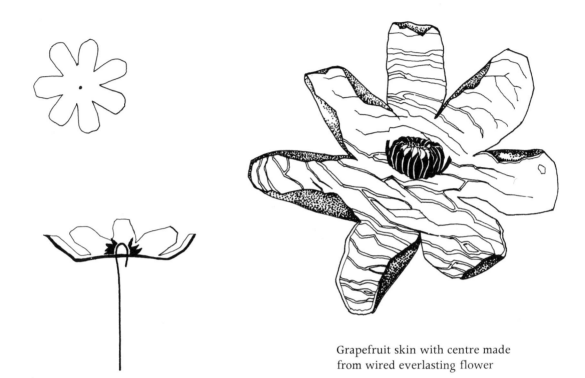

Grapefruit skin with centre made
from wired everlasting flower

gent can be made into a stiff paste with water and will be quite secure. This last method involves working at speed, as it sets quickly. The whiteness of the plaster can be camouflaged by rubbing it over with brown shoe polish when dry.

Water-retaining blocks, such as *Oasis* (used dry), are good, and blocks of dry foam, such as *Prestige*, or *Styrofoam* are sold specially for dried arrangements. Both need to be firmly fixed to the container, either on special holders or pinholders, as they are light and the weight of the arrangement can easily over-balance them. I often use a block of foam on a holder, and then cover it with 50 mm (2 in.) mesh

43

wire netting, fixed firmly to the container, to secure heavy stems. A really large dried group may also need a small weight hidden at the back of the container.

Sometimes it makes a change to mix some fresh flowers or foliage with the dried pieces. Bronze chrysanthemums look attractive with copper or glycerined beach, and many a tired arrangement can be resurrected in the spring by the addition of irises or daffodils. When mixing these two kinds of plant material, care must be taken to seal the stems of the dried ones, especially bullrushes which will 'blow' in water. This can be done in several ways: single stems can be coated with a thick layer of varnish or sealed with sticky tape; while a group can go in a polythene bag. Sometimes it is possible to insert one container inside another and to keep one wet and one dry. Of course, if the dried material has false stems, there is no problem.

I enlarge on the subject of containers on pages 70 to 77 but I would emphasize that it is not essential to use expensive or exotic bowls or vases. Of course it is fun to collect interesting containers, since these add to the beauty of the arrangement, but it is also possible to produce a most pleasing effect in something very simple.

I have a beautiful tall cylindrical vase which came from Thailand, lacquered in black and decorated in gold leaf. I use it for a very simple vertical arrangement which includes *Acanthus,* leek seedheads, *Delphinium* seedheads, the leaves of *Rhododendrons* and *Achillea* – all home grown and home dried. It is given a touch of glamour by the addition of some *Proteas*, which also pick up the gold in the decoration. The arrangement is secured in 50 mm (2 in.) mesh wire netting which has been crumpled into a roll and inserted deep into the container. For safety, a small weight is suspended from the back to balance the tall vase and heavy seedheads. Special weights may be bought for this purpose, or some soft lead rolled into a length and tucked inside the neck of the vase at the back.

14   Dried material in Thai vase

Another of my collected pieces is a spelter figurine called *Joyeuse Fermiere*, bought in France very cheaply, but minus the top of the arm. The fact that this was missing not only reduced the price but was highly convenient, because my husband was able to convert it into a container by screwing a tin onto the broken part. He also added a small wooden base to improve the balance; and I changed the whole thing from a rather miserable grey to russet brown with shoe polish. A block of foam fixed in the tin with sticky tape holds the arrangement, which is light and quite safe. The plant material consists of seedheads of plantain, *Allium, Nigella, Iris, Moluccella*, cotton (picked up in Greece) with *Eucalyptus* and *Aspidistra* leaves.

◀ 15   Dried and preserved material
in spelter figurine

I also have two Victorian glass domes; the small one has been used for a colourful arrangement of material preserved in borax, and the large one has more unusual dried material, most of it imported from abroad.

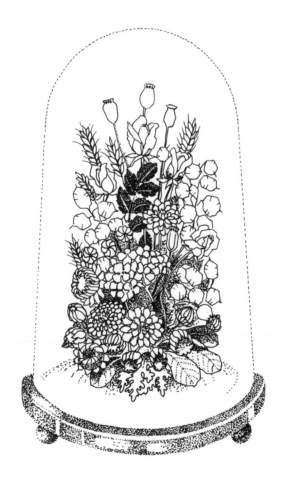

16 Victorian glass dome with imported dried material

17 Victorian glass dome arrangement

Candlesticks make very attractive containers for dried arrangements. Special metal bowls called *candlecups* can be bought to insert into the candle holder, but just a ring of *Plasticine* is often sufficient when water is not required. I have made a simple arrangement in an old brass candlestick by surrounding a dull yellow candle (which goes very well with the brass) with *Plasticine*, and inserting into this a few stems of *Moluccella* and some glycerined beech leaves (Colour plate 2).

I made an attractive table arrangement in an old discarded pendant candelabra which had held electric light bulbs. It was glued onto a wooden base and a small tin screwed to the top. The whole thing was sprayed with bronze, plus a touch of black while the paint was still wet, to dull it down a little. Candles went into the spaces which held the bulbs, and a dried arrangement of pampas grass, *Achillea*, thistle and *Protea* in the middle. At Christmas I use holly with red candles.

18   Arrangement of grasses and *Helichrysums* in plastic goblet

Overleaf
19   Table centre made from old electric light pendant
20   Plastic gilt candlestick with gilded arrangement of *Mahonia* leaves, pampas grass, *Astrantia* and poppy seedheads

Cones are best made in dry foam; it can be bought all ready in cone-shaped pieces. Or, small crumbs of old foam can be hoarded, kept dry and then stuffed into a wire cage. The wire cages, too, can be bought in cone shapes and are very firm and good to use. But if the cone is to be given as a gift, it is a bit extravagant to give away a fairly expensive wire cone – so I sometimes make mine from 15 mm ($\frac{1}{2}$ in.) mesh wire netting.

I first cut a pattern from newspaper, to make a cornet when folded. Transfer this on top of the wire and cut it with wire-cutters. The wire cone is then lined with the newspaper and stuffed with the small crumbs of foam which would otherwise be wasted. I seal the base with silver foil and place the cone on a pedestal-type container. That is, one with a short stem, as this seems to show off the finished cone to greater advantage. A fruit compote will fulfil the same purpose.

Start at the base with some flat leaves, to make a sort of collar, but vary the lengths of the stems so that this collar is not too uniform. Turn the cone while working so that it is similar all round. Now change to rounded material and work towards the top. Small poppy seedheads, beech nuts, *Helichrysums* to give colour, *Achillea*, small clusters of *Hydrangea* heads, cones and berries are just a few of the suitable materials. Use shorter stems towards the top; indeed, none of the stems should be more than 50 mm (2 in.) even at the base, and it is important to keep a good graduated shape throughout. A small spiky piece can be put at the very top to emphasise the shape. See also colour plate 1.

21   Made up cone with mixture of dried and plastic material

54

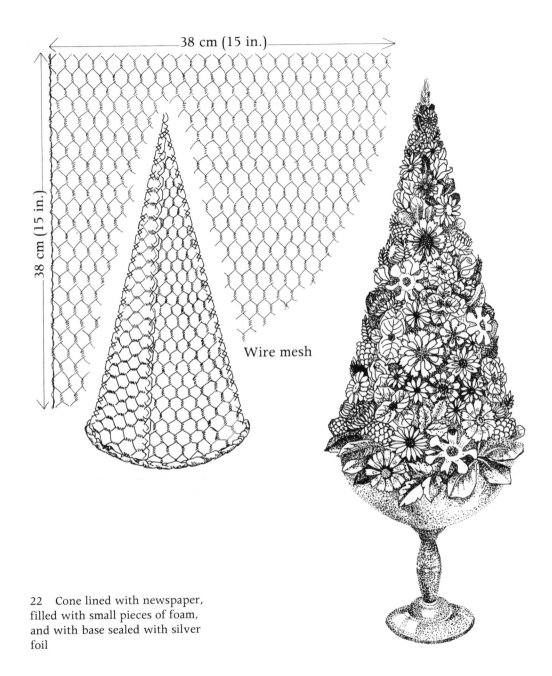

38 cm (15 in.)

38 cm (15 in.)

Wire mesh

22   Cone lined with newspaper,
filled with small pieces of foam,
and with base sealed with silver
foil

55

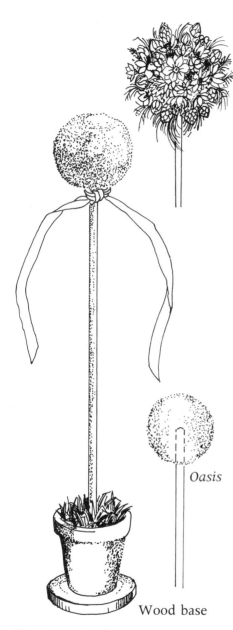

A pot tree is effective and very simple to make. First, attach a plastic flower pot to a round wooden base about a third larger than the smallest diameter of the pot. I use *Araldite* for this; the base adds considerably to the stability of the finished product. Dried material is light and does not have the added weight of water. I line the bottom of the pot with newspaper and small heavy stones before filling it to within 25 mm (1 in.) of the top with plaster filling or cement. A thin rod about three-and-a-half times the height of the pot is placed in the centre and the cement is then left to set. Keep an eye on it while it is setting so that the rod does not slip off centre. The height and thickness of the rod must always be in proportion to the size of the pot – I have used tiny sticks inside yoghourt pots for table decorations, and large broomsticks inside tubs to stand at a doorway. The larger trees may not, of course, require the extra base. Spear a ball of foam to the top of the rod, and be careful not to allow it to go right through or the ball will slip down when full. It can be prevented from doing this by winding some string a few times around the rod directly underneath the ball of foam. A round ball of mesh wire is equally suitable for dried material, and a ball of moss can be used for fresh flowers.

Start at the base with rather flat foliage – *Cupresses* is good – to make a kind of frill, but try not to get this looking too much like a collar. Varying the lengths of the stems will help. Now work up and round the ball, keeping a rounded shape all the time. This means that all the stems must now be cut the same length and mostly rounded material should be used – *Helichrysums*, *Hydrangea* clusters, *Nigella* seedheads, cones, poppy seedheads, etc. But the ball may be varied with a few pieces of spiked material (so long as it is not too heavy) like *Solidago* or many of the grasses.

I usually paint the pot and rod to blend with the arrangement. Brown or bronze looks good with a toning ribbon streamer directly underneath the ball of flowers.

Oasis

Wood base

23   Preparation for pot tree

Gourds

It is a little difficult to use gourds as they are extremely hard when properly ripe. They should be varnished with artist's colourless varnish and can be used in large garlands or swags. Alternatively, a simple bowl, especially if it is copper or brass, can look most attractive if piled high with gourds in different colours. To vary the height in the bowl, and so that all the gourds will be visible, some of them may need to be raised.

Small rings of cardboard will achieve this; or, if the bowl is to have a few preserved leaves added, small mesh wire can be put underneath. This will serve the dual purpose of raising the height of the gourds and providing a foundation for the stems of the leaves.

Swags

For a Grinling Gibbons type of wall swag, make a roll of 50 mm (2 in.) mesh wire netting about 455 mm (18 in.) shorter than the required length when completed. This may be backed either with a piece of foam rubber or enclosed in a nylon stocking to protect the wall when it is put in place. Another idea is to attach the wire roll to a narrow board which has already been covered with fabric. Tweed or hessian is suitable for dried swags, though they can look lovely too on velvet. The dried material is then inserted into the wire which will hold it quite safely. The swag must be wide at the top and taper towards the base, and a variety of material can be used. Flat, fairly pointed, wide leaves are necessary at the top and small ones at the base. A swag can be made to look very colourful. I have done one with the dried skins of citrus fruits, *Helichrysums*

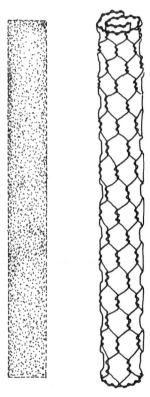

Foam rubber
50 mm (2 in.) mesh wire
Board covered with fabric

57

and the seedheads of *Iris foetidissima* – all of which give a vivid touch of orange and yellow. Bleached *Hydrangea* heads, small cones and lily (*martagon*) seedheads are added, and the final swag attached to a board covered with dark muted green tweed. The *Iris* seedheads and any other soft berries must be sprayed with colourless hair lacquer to preserve their life, but even then they will not last as long as some of the other material. See colour plate 4.

Another type of swag may be made as a ring and it can be mounted on a wire coat-hanger. Pull this into a circle, preserving the hook, which will be useful to suspend the finished swag, and cover the wire with brown crêpe paper. Then bind the dried pieces on with reel wire. This makes a thin and delicate ring, but it can be thickened by rolling 50 mm (2 in.) mesh wire netting into a circle, or binding *Oasis* or dry foam to the ring.

A long swag, to be draped over a mantlepiece or down either side of a door is best made with a more pliable foundation. Mesh wire is too stiff. Nylon stockings filled with oddments of *Oasis* or dry foam may be used, or the stockings filled with rolled-up newspaper. For this, it will be necessary to bind the material on with reel wire as it will not be easy to push the stems into the newspaper. Remember to anchor one end before starting work!

Hanging arrangements can be made in so many ways, starting with a simple ball of dry foam or *Oasis*, covered in silver foil. Push a hole right through this and insert a toning ribbon with which to suspend the ball. Make the holes for the material with a skewer, otherwise the stems may break. Just cover it completely with rounded pieces.

Any shallow wicker or cane trays can be made into wall arrangements by putting a wire through at the top to form a hook and wiring a block of foam, *Plasticine*, or a ball of wire towards the base. Make sure the holding agent is firmly fixed before starting work by passing reel wire over the top and through the basket to the back.

24 Swag

25 Arrangement on wicker rice
basket from Thailand *Achillea,
Aspidistra*, pampas grass,
Helichrysums and *Iris* and *Nigella*
seedheads
26 Plaque with grasses and
Helipterum
27 Simple plaque with *Grevillea*
fern (glycerined), dried hare's
tail grass and *Helichrysum*

59

Cakeboards can be covered with oddments of fabric and made into delightful wall decorations (figure 24). A firmer base can be made with a piece of hardboard; a cameo style arrangement will result if this is cut into an oval shape. Cover the board with the chosen material; make small holes for the binding wire and for wire to form a hook; then cover the back with cardboard to neaten it off. A tapering arrangement, designed to fill one side, or an arrangement to come up from the base in a crescent shape, will complete the cameo effect.

Overleaf
30   Arrangement in cupid
figurine with *Helichrysums,* hare's
tail grasses and *Astilbe*

31   Sunburst
Wall decoration of imported dyed
materials

A border of dried material can look attractive round a mirror (figure 29), and an old picture frame can be used also in this way. Gilt frames look delightful if the arrangement is made inside the frame on a velvet or hessian backing and left without glass. It should be wired on in the same way as the plaque.

Of course, it is possible to do very beautiful designs with some of the dried material which is imported from South America, Japan and other countries. I have included some illustrations of arrangements made with this. Much of it is artificially coloured, but as this is now allowed in competitive flower shows, busy arrangers may be pleased to use it occasionally. I find I can get very good subtle shades by dyeing my own natural-coloured material with *Dylon* dyes. I use the hot water method and vary the colour by the time of immersion in the dye solution.

28   Plaque with *Helichrysum*
Facing page
29   Dried swag around a mirror

Adapting for Christmas

The basic requirements for transforming dried arrangements into sparkling Christmas decorations are very simple: aerosol cans of paint in gold, silver and copper; various tubes of glitter; and some ribbons and baubles.

Be discerning with both glitter and paint; many things will be greatly enhanced by just a touch of colour, but heavy spraying gives results which are flat and clumsy. Often no paint is needed at all, but just a smear of colourless glue and a sprinkle of glitter. Honesty seedpods are charming if only the edge is touched with glitter; and gold glitter on the edges of tiny cones looks very attractive. Poppy seedheads can be sprayed with paint and the flat top centre – but only this part – glittered. Most of the everlastings need only a spot of glitter in the centre – they have enough colour of their own.

Many of the dried arrangements can be sprayed and glittered complete. To do this, line a deep sink or a box with newspaper, place the arrangement inside, and spray. If separate odd pieces are placed underneath, this will economise on spray. The easiest and most economical way to use glitter is to put it into a polythene bag (without holes!) and to dip the flower or leaf into the bag while it is still wet with paint or glue; though of course this is not possible with complete arrangements.

Facing page
32   Door circle for Christmas
A mixture of walnuts, seedheads and plastic fruits

PLATE 3

Pressed flower picture

Dried flower picture J Middleditch

Hanging arrangements can be made to look more seasonable by the addition of bells, baubles and ribbon bows. If one is designed for the front door, be sure to use waterproof ribbon. The little pot trees may have stemmed baubles inserted between the dried material, and the pot and rod can be sprayed silver, gold or copper. Garlands can be enlivened with small sprigs of holly here and there, or tiny plastic fruits. This is the one time of year when even flower arrangers can use plastic without flinching! White plastic Christmas roses (*Helleborus*) and tiny grapes can be used with great effect. I have made a door garland with dried material, brightened with tiny plastic oranges, lemons and grapes, Christmas roses and green velvet ribbon. I added some walnuts which have a good rough texture and can be easily attached by passing a strand of reel wire around the join of the nut. Quite a change from the usual holly wreath. A dried cone was brightened by inserting a few plastic fruits and then lightly sprayed with copper, but not glittered. Two small circles were made of matching material to fit around small candle-holders, and candles picking up one of the colours of the fruit were placed either side of the cone for a table decoration (figure 37).

Two circles of dried material can be made on wire or wire coat-hangers, tied inside each other to form a kissing ring, then sprayed with paint.

The garden hanging basket which has been put away for the winter can also be filled with an assortment of dried material. Line it first with silver foil or polythene and push some of the material down through the foil and out of the base of the basket, before spraying gold or silver. Add some ribbon bows or baubles. Sometimes a good result is obtained by mixing the paint (eg gold and silver; copper and silver) preferably while still wet. A muted arrangement in a candle stick can be transformed at Christmas by changing the colour of the candles and adding a touch of paint in the same colour. Candles can improve many an arrangement;

Facing page
33 Arrangement on cake pedestal with skeleton *Magnolia* leaves, *Helipterum*, various small seed-heads and glass baubles, all silvered and glittered

67

34　A cracker and a made-up
flower
Flower is skeletonised *Magnolia*
leaves with poppyhead centre
Cracker is a cardboard cylinder
from paper towels, covered in gold
foil with arrangement of small
dried and glycerined seedheads

35　Decorated Christmas parcel

one way of inserting a candle into foam is to sticky tape three hairpin pieces of wire to the base, with a short leg of wire protruding. This will stay firmly in place without making too big a hole in the foam; or it will go into a pin-holder. If a more natural look is required for Christmas, group some cones on a piece of wood; use bullrushes for height, skeleton magnolia leaves for lightness; and a few pieces of ivy – lightly glittered – around the edges.

A vertical arrangement in the black and gold Thai vase (figure 14) was made to look glamorous for Christmas by spraying some of the material gold, with the addition of a few gold foil leaves. Small arrangements make delightful gifts if fixed, with plaster filling, into scallop shells or cream or yoghourt cartons. I find it best to complete the arrangement and allow it to set before spraying the whole thing.

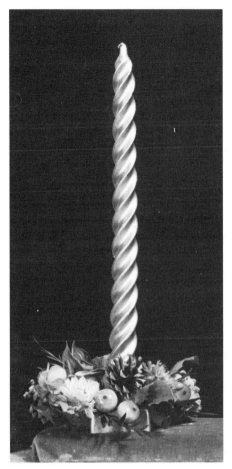

36 Dried pot tree glittered for Christmas

37 One of the candles for table decoration

69

Containers

Vases or *bowls* to the uninitiated, but *containers* to the flower arranger! The technical difference between a vase and a bowl is that the vase has a height greater than its circumference, and a bowl a width greater than its height; but the use of the general word container covers anything.

The right container is a very important factor in the success of any flower arrangement, and especially so with dried or preserved material. It forms part of the whole in the same way that a frame does with a picture. This does not mean that exotic or expensive containers are essential to good flower arranging, merely that they must be right for the job they have to do.

On the whole, glass is seldom suitable for dried arrangements; but all kinds of heavy pottery, particularly in soft modern muted glazes and severe functional shapes, lend themselves well to dried flowers. Pewter, brass and copper look good whether in jugs, dishes, plates or trays; and it is often possible to pick up the colour of the metal with some of the dried material. Basketware in rush or wicker is fine, and so is any kind of wooden container. A wooden cheese or breadboard, a wooden plate or a flat slice of wood which has been specially prepared, all make exceptionally good bases for dried material. Shells are another idea and are useful for daintier stems; so are small flat pieces of fungi, dried hard. Arrangements can be fixed on most of these by means of a block of *Plasticine*. A fairly safe guide to the type of container to use is to avoid anything too sophisticated or with a high sheen or gloss.

A round or square cakeboard or an oval piece of hardboard can be covered with velvet or any plain surfaced material for a base, or – as described earlier – to make a hanging arrangement. Oddments of fabric picked up on the remnant counter are useful for this. Cut the fabric about 75 mm (3 in.) wider than the base to be used, then glue the edges with *Copydex*, pulling it tight to avoid wrinkles. Weight it down firmly until it is set, then neaten off the back with a circle of cardboard to hide the rough edges. Sometimes a strip of narrow braid is glued round the rim. If the arrangement is intended to be a hanging one, do not forget to put on the hook before finishing it off. A set of three bases, each about one inch smaller than the other and covered in the same fabric, make an attractive stepped base. It is best to use a pinholder in a dish on these covered bases as *Plasticine* will mark the fabric.

All kinds of containers can be made at very little cost; and, as the arrangement does not need water, it is not necessary to make sure they are waterproof.

A plastic washing-up liquid holder makes a very good Japanese-style vase if the top is cut off neatly and the outside covered with a rough plaster mixture. It can then be spray painted or left in its natural creamy-white state. It is necessary with this – as with all light-weight jars – to put a few handfuls of sand or stones in the base for stability. Another idea is to wind rough string around the outside in a tight neat spiral. There is available a wide variety of self-adhesive paper in simulated wood, mosaic, bamboo, etc. I have rolled a plastic holder in glue and then sand before painting it, with interesting results. It is very important to use flat paint, either undercoat or a matt finish. To colour my plaster-covered containers, I mix a few drops of

38　Home-made containers
Washing-up liquid holder covered
with rough plaster
Gilt cupid with small glass phial
on plaster base
Large cream carton, inverted, with
small plastic bowl glued to top
Gilded coffee jar covered with
sand and small stones

vegetable colouring, bought for cooking, with the plaster
mixture. I have covered the outside of a bottle with this
mixture. And, of course, it is possible to get all kinds of
colours by experimenting. A tiny perfume bottle was
covered this way, then stuck onto a base of the same
plaster mixture, with a small gold cupid attached to the
bottle.

Shallow containers can be made from the small cardboard
dishes used for pre-packed fruit and vegetables or from
lids of boxes. I cover these with silver foil, wrong side out,
to give added firmness, and make a rather liquid plaster

mixture which I run all over the base and sides. To make a larger shallow dish, cut a piece of cardboard into an irregular oval, then place it on a piece of 15 mm ($\frac{1}{2}$ in.) mesh wire netting. Turn up the edge of the wire and cardboard and then cover the whole thing with foil before running a rather thicker plaster mixture all over it. The base needs to be fairly smooth, but the sides can be as rough as taste dictates. When it is quite dry and set, run a coat of clear varnish or sealer over the base; though it does not matter if these containers are not completely waterproof.

39 Home-made containers
Cardboard dish, bottles and tin pie dish before and after covering with plaster mixture

74

Even if they are used for fresh flowers, a well pinholder or an ordinary pinholder in a small dish can be placed inside them. Small tins which have held steak and kidney pies make good containers – but watch for rust! This type of tin is often useful to attach, by screw or solder, on to a figurine or a pedestal type lamp-holder. Do not disdain garish china at a jumble sale – the *shape* is the important thing, and any pattern or vivid colour can be disguised with paint. A rough piece of slate makes a lovely base for dried arrangements, and some interesting pieces of wood can often be found – tree bark, for instance. Most dried things look charming on wood and can be varied in the spring by adding another small container with a few fresh flowers – daffodils or perhaps the first primroses or snowdrops.

40 Arrangement using centre container shown in figure 39

41 Arrangement on dried oyster fungi

75

42　Small basket with arrangement of lotus and leek seedheads

If a slice of wood can be found at a sawmill, be careful to get well-seasoned wood which will not split when brought into the warmth of the house. Treat it with linseed oil for protection, and then a very light application of furniture polish, enough to bring out the beauty of the grain but not to make it shiny. It can be varnished to protect it from dampness, but personally I prefer to risk this and to keep the wood looking as natural as possible. I usually attach a backing of felt to protect the surface on which it will stand. Heavy ivy or heather root, drift-wood, fungi, etc, can all be used as containers. They all need to be well cleaned, and possibly treated with an anti-woodworm mixture. Sometimes they can be screwed on to another firm base or kept in place with a plaster mixture, with a small bowl or tin attached to take the arrangement; but for dried arrangements, *Plasticine* will be sufficient.

Another easy idea is to use straw-covered bottles, or candlesticks with a wedge of *Plasticine* on the top, to make attractive holders, with or without a candle.

Pressed flower pictures

A further development of the use of dried material is to make pictures with pressed flowers. These were very popular with the Victorians who produced some charming, if slightly overcrowded, results. Today we are rather more restrained, and skill as a flower arranger will contribute to the perfection of the finished picture. Of course, beautiful pictures are produced, too, by people who have never arranged a flower in their lives, but who already possess a good sense of design. And not only pictures. Calendars, finger-plates for doors, table-mats and so on – all can be made with that personal touch which preserves the beauty of the hedge and garden.

The bare necessities for this work are simple. First, a wooden frame for pressing the plant material. *Two* wooden frames are even better because it is useful to have a small one to take on holiday, in the car, and for walks. The sooner the material is pressed after picking, the better it will be. Yet, a frame is not absolutely essential – the job can be done with a large pile of heavy books; but this takes more room and more time. I find, too, that the colours are not so good when the pressing process takes a longer time.

For the larger press, cut a piece of 7-ply plywood into two oblong bits, each about 205 mm × 254 mm (8 in. × 10 in.). Smooth the wood and round off the corners. Bore

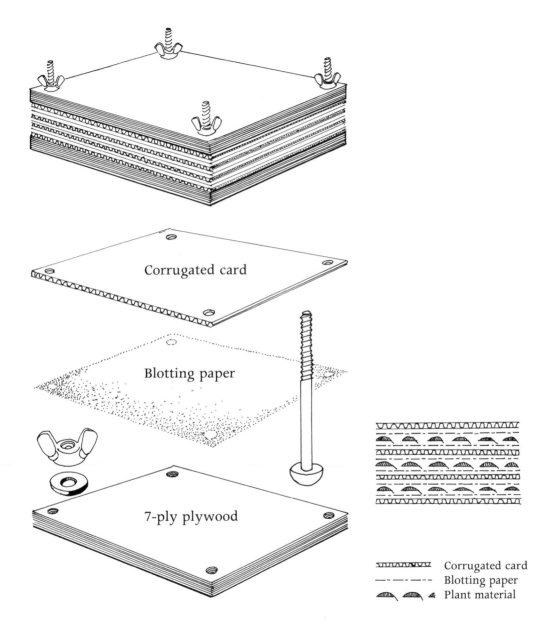

Corrugated card

Blotting paper

7-ply plywood

〰〰〰〰〰 Corrugated card
— — — — — Blotting paper
🐛 🐛 🐚 Plant material

43   Flower press

a hole a 6 mm ($\frac{1}{4}$ in.) in diameter about 15 mm ($\frac{1}{2}$ in.) from each corner (see figure 43) and insert four bolts 65 mm ($2\frac{1}{2}$ in.) long × 6 mm ($\frac{1}{4}$ in.) thick. Buy these complete with wing-nuts. Cut thick cardboard – corrugated is best – and blotting paper the same size as the wood, and make matching holes in the corner of each piece. It is useful to strengthen these with ring reinforcements so that they do not break away too easily. About twenty pieces of blotting paper and ten of cardboard will be needed.

A fairly large heavy book (old telephone directories are fine) is necessary as well to store the pressed material prior to use. Art paper or backing board is required for making the picture – this is easily obtainable from any art shop or good stationer's. Heavy cardboard or hardboard for backing, heavy brown paper or thin cardboard, panel pins, nylon cord, glue (I use *Copydex*), and of course frames, complete the list.

It is possible, if making only one or two pictures, to take the finished design to an art shop and have it framed professionally. But this is rather an expensive business, though it looks delightful and beautifully finished.

I have found a great deal of pleasure in hunting for old frames for my pictures, either in jumble sales, junk shops, furniture sales or the many 'charity' shops throughout the country. It is an added challenge to design a picture which is right for a particular frame and this adds greatly to the joy of the finished product. It is possible, too, to make frames at home from picture framing bought at an art shop, and to get glass cut to fit.

Old frames need some preparation before they are ready for use. The whole thing must be taken to pieces (watch for woodworm) and the glass removed. The glass needs a good clean on both sides, and any rusty hooks and panel pins taken out. Clean up the frame well – I sometimes paint mine with gold, silver or copper if the wood is dull and worn; this can really glamorise most old frames.

PLATE 4

Christmas swag.
Mixture of dried material sprayed with gold paint   Flowers preserved in borax

44 Plant material on blotting
paper in press

Table mat

Having done all this, I then cut a piece of whatever art paper I have chosen to the exact size of the glass. I use various colours for backing, but seldom anything too vivid. The plant material is rather muted and must not be overshadowed by the background. One exception is grey leaves and white flowers, which look startling on a scarlet backing. It is best to use a flat-surfaced paper always, and to avoid anything with a shine or gloss. Black is always successful, and it is possible to find a flocked paper which looks exactly like velvet. Indeed, there seems to be no reason why oddments of velvet could not be used as backings. It would need to be stretched very neatly and tidily, but should look rather beautiful. If the picture is designed for a particular room, the colour scheme of that room could be picked up in the backing as well as in the pressed material in the picture.

If the frames need glass, now is the time to get it cut – do not wait until the picture is finished. (In fact, it is best to prepare everything needed before starting work.) Table mats need heavy heat-proof glass, *Perspex* or *Plexiglass*; calendars or bookmarks can be covered in thin or clear plastic and stuck on to coarse linen, crash or ribbon. None of the pictures must be mounted, as the design has to be in close contact with the glass. The material to be pressed must be as perfect as possible; it should not be picked when wet, and any damaged leaves or petals eaten by insects must be discarded.

Immediately the press is ready, whatever the time of year, it is possible to find something in the garden or hedge. Often it may be more convenient to carry with you a small plastic bag rather than the press; when this is filled it can be secured with an elastic band. By pressing all the year round, it is possible to find an enormous variety of shapes, colours and textures, and to experiment as flowers and foliage become available. Some things will obviously be more successful than others; the failures can be thrown away.

A general guide is that flat flowers (eg the daisy or viola families) are very easy and successful. Any large flower heads must be pulled gently apart and each petal pressed separately. *Hydrangea,* for instance, must be cut into individual florets (or bracts), but these look lovely when done, especially the greenish colours. Most of the *Clematis* are beautiful; again, each petal of the larger varieties must be done separately – they can often be used on the reverse side which sometimes has attractive marking. The tendrils of the *Clematis* should be included to give interesting shapes. *Astrantia maxima* looks very exotic and can be used either by itself or to make the centre of a made-up flower. *Alchemilla mollis* (ladies' mantle) provides a touch of daintiness, as does *Gypsophila* (baby's breath). The purple flowers of *Lunaria* (honesty) look exactly like violets when pressed. Cornflowers and *Delphiniums* (each floret pressed separately in *Delphiniums*) are a lovely shade of blue which they keep when finished.

Remember that everything is going to lose some of the colour, but this will not detract from the subtle charm of the finished article. It is as well not to hang the picture in full sun. This avoids the loss of colour for as long as possible; it is worth noting that yellows and blues keep their colour the longest. Most of the everlasting flowers are good because they keep their true colours quite a long time; but choose the finer kind, like *Helipterum*. Many of the buttercup family are successful and the colour lasts well. These can be pressed open or flat, together with the stalk. The *Umbelliferae* (parsley) family and the fluffy seedheads of wild *Clematis vitalba* (traveller's joy) are beautiful; rose petals provide a delightful satin texture, though they do not keep their colour very well. Some spiky material must be included. Heaths are suitable and, of course, grasses. Pick these, unlike the flowers, complete with stalk. From grasses to foliage of all kinds: *Adiantum* (maidenhair fern) is very delicate; ivy of many species has a good shape but

Stylised design

cannot be relied upon to keep green. However, it turns to a very pleasant brown, so long as this is kept in mind when planning the final colour scheme. Much of the grey foliage is excellent – *Cineraria maritima* (sea ragwort) and *Senecio greyi*, also the reverse side of the leaf of whitebeam. Some *Clematis* leaves dry black and make a very good contrast; many *Acer* leaves have good shapes. The *Cornus* (dogwood) and *Hypericum* (St John's wort) are pretty, and, in the autumn, beech and blackberry just turning colour. These may be brittle when dried and need careful handling.

Have the press filled all the time; as one batch matures and is transferred to the storage book, fill it with fresh material so that there is always a good selection when needed. Stalks must not be forgotten, preferably thin ones like buttercups or primroses. If thicker stalks are required, hunt for something soft as hard stems are difficult to press and use in a picture.

There is a list of plant material on page 88, all of which I have tried and found suitable, but there will also be many other things which will do well. Start pressing round about February and go on throughout the year, experimenting with various shapes, colours and textures.

Having collected the plant material, insert the bolts from underneath the wooden frame and place one sheet of blotting paper on this. Arrange the specimens carefully on it, spreading out the petals and leaves, face downwards where possible. A small soft brush will help here as the specimens must not be torn or damaged in any way. Discard anything which is not almost perfect; I say 'almost' as sometimes a slightly off-centre petal or leaf can give a much more natural look to a design. But plant material eaten by insects or otherwise too disfigured is not suitable. Do not allow any of the petals to overlap, and be sure nothing comes over the side of the press. Curve some of the stems slightly – a strip of *Sellotape* or *Scotch Tape* will help to do this, or a pin at a strategic point (but be careful that the point does not penetrate the blotting paper layer). When the sheet is full, cover it with another piece of blotting paper and then a sheet of cardboard. Repeat these sandwiches until the press is full, finishing with cardboard. Then put on the other piece of wood and secure the press with the washers and wing-nuts on the top. Tighten each nut gently until it is as tight as possible. As the plant material settles down, the nuts will loosen and the slack should be taken up. A warning note here: very delicate petals and leaves should either be done separately, with the pressure somewhat lightened, or pressed between blotting paper and heavy books. Too much pressure can shatter fragile flowers.

After twenty-four hours, the press must be opened very carefully and the specimens removed, put on to fresh blotting paper and then re-assembled for another forty-eight hours. The press should always be stored, meanwhile, out of the damp and draughts, but not anywhere too hot. The material is then ready for use.

However, it will not all be required at once, and this is where the heavy book comes in. Transfer the pressed material, very gently, to this storage book and be careful to keep colours together. Group leaves, stalks and grasses and if anything feels the slightest bit damp, put it between blotting paper, too, while in the storage book. It is also essential to place a marker in each page, with a note of colour and contents. If this is not done, it can lead to chaos when assembling material for a picture.

Be careful to store everything flat and uncreased; for this reason it is easier to start at the back of the book so that no pages are disturbed as the work proceeds. Secure the book with a large elastic band or tape and put it away – again out of the damp – until required. Fresh material can be added as and when collected and pressed; the more there is, the better.

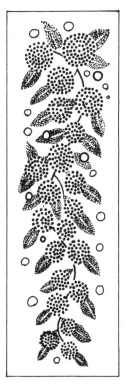

Finger plate

To make a picture

Decide on the colour scheme, taking into consideration the plant material, the frame, the backing, and the destination of the picture, if known. There is a great variety in the colours in which backing paper can be obtained, and it is interesting to experiment with these. Most good art shops will have a selection.

Many of the yellow and orange flowers are shown to advantage on a soft brown or coffee-coloured backing; mauves and blues go very well on grey; pink is pretty on pale green; and most things, except of course white, look good on white. Black is nearly always successful, though it does need careful handling as every small blemish shows. Marry the frame with the backing: for instance, a silver frame asks for grey or white; copper goes well with a brown background; and white and black are striking with gilt frames.

Cut the chosen backing paper and the cardboard or hardboard to the same size as the glass and make sure it fits neatly and tightly into the frame. Cut the brown paper the same size as the frame itself, with very neat edges. Have ready some glue (*Copydex* is good) and a small soft paint-brush.

It will help if at first the design is planned on a piece of plain paper cut the same size as the glass, though with experience this is not necessary, and it will be possible to assemble the picture directly on to the final backing. The shape and design will be governed by the shape and size of the frame (see sketches), and there are endless variations possible, according to taste and ability. A natural style may be chosen, making the plant material look almost as though it is growing, or a more stylised pattern may be preferred. Also keep on hand a large sheet of glass to cover the material in preparation in case it has to be left – an open window or draught from a door can cause havoc to a design which has been carefully put in place but not yet stuck down. And, as always, it must be kept quite free from all dampness.

It is best to fill at least two-thirds of the space in the frame to avoid an empty look, but do not be tempted to overcrowd the picture and confuse the line. A gentle curve towards the tip, using heavy material, and the larger flowers and leaves at the base allowing each specimen to be seen clearly, is far more effective than a mass jumbled together. I have seen many flower pictures with beautiful material, where the artist has tried obviously to include something of everything; so I feel very strongly that some real design must be attempted to make a successful picture. It is sometimes easier to space out the chosen pattern by placing stalks in position first, and then adding flowers and leaves in proportion. Small items, such as heartsease pansies and field daisies, are best for narrow small frames, while heavier flowers need frames to scale. Separate petals may be combined to make an exotic flower with no name – rose or tulip petals with a tiny daisy for the centre, for instance.

When the design is satisfactory, start to transfer it to the backing. When the stalks are in place, work from the top downwards; this will avoid damage to the completed part. Just touch the back of each petal or leaf with glue, using a soft brush or a small spatula. Apply the glue mainly to the base of the petals unless they are large, when they will need a touch at the tip as well. Use glue sparingly on the stalks, but be sure to put some at each end and in the middle, to secure it firmly. Mistakes are not important; *Copydex* can be removed without making a mark, and it is useful to keep a box of tissues handy for this purpose. Make sure that no surplus glue is left on the surface and that the inside of the glass is clean. Do not be tempted to use up that odd flower; remember the trite but true maxim, 'When in doubt, leave it out'.

Initial or sign the picture now. Then place the finished design on the glass, back it with the heavy cardboard or hardboard and press this firmly against the picture. It must not move about or the air will penetrate and spoil the colours and the material very quickly. Be careful to get it all just right and see that there are no specks of dirt in the finished pattern. Secure the whole thing with panel pins, then paste the heavy brown paper or thin cardboard – cut exactly the size of the *outside* of the frame this time – over the back to give a neat finish. It adds interest to list on the back of each picture the materials used, before attaching two rings and a nylon cord to complete the work.

Suggestions of material to press for pictures

Listed under names most commonly in use – not necessarily the Latin ones.

FLOWERS

Alchemilla mollis
Anaphalis
Astilibe
Astrantia maxima
Buttercups and *ranunculas*
Clematis
Cornflower
Cranesbill
Daisy (wild ones are very good)

Daisy *Anthemis cupaniana*
Delphinium
Geum
Golden rod – variety *goldenmosa*
Heaths
Helipterum
Heuchera
Helleborus
Honesty
Honeysuckle
Hydrangea
Montbretia
Nepeta
Star of Bethlehem
Viola (pansy) (mostly yellow and dark colours; also tiny heartsease)
Wild parsley of all kinds
FOLIAGE
Acer
Adiantum
Aspen
Beech
Blackberry
Cineraria maritima – variety *candicans*
Clematis
Cornus
Hedera
Helleborus
Pyrethrum Parthenium (feverfew)
Raspberry
Senecio greyi
Tiarella
Whitebeam
Yarrow
Also many ferns and grasses
Stalks

45   Natural design

Further ideas

Crystalised flowers

Suitable flowers for this purpose: violets, primroses, mimosa, cowslips, apple blossom – but try anything sweet-scented. Shadow leaves may be done by a method of dipping them in egg white and castor sugar.

Put 3 teaspoonsful of gum arabic (crystals) in a small screw-top jar with a lid. Cover these with 3 tablespoonsful of rose or orange water. Leave for 3 days, shaking occasionally.

This will now be a sticky substance. Using a soft paintbrush, coat petals, calyx and some of the stem of each flower (if required). Take more intricate flowers apart and coat the petals individually. Do not miss any part or this will shrivel. Dredge with castor sugar until well covered, then dry off in a warm place (the linen cupboard is ideal). After about 24 hours the flowers should be dry and stiff. Store away in the dark.

Rose petal jam

1·1365 litres (2 pints) rose petals (strongly scented – dark red are good)
·907 kg (2 lb) cube sugar
1·1365 litres (2 pints) setting fluid (*Certo* or similar)
Juice of a lemon.

Take off the white base of the petal. Mix petals and sugar and leave for about 12 hours. Then put into a pan and bring slowly to the boil. Add Certo. Fast boil for 10 minutes or until set.

Drying the skins of fruit and vegetables

As I needed some colour for a swag I was once making, I decided to experiment with the skins of various fruits and vegetables. I found that citrus fruits were most successful and supplied a vivid touch of colour. Oranges, lemons, lime and grapefruit were included. It is necessary to peel the fruit carefully. Strip away all the membrane from the inside very gently, being sure not to break the skin if possible; I scrape mine with a small knife. The orange can sometimes be peeled whole to make a four-petalled flower complete, but most of the skin can be cut into petal or leaf shapes. Make a small hole at the base of each piece before drying – it is for the mounting wire, because the skin will be too dry to do this afterwards.

Leave the shaped pieces somewhere warm but not too hot. Between the oven and the grill (when the oven is on but the grill is not!) is a good place, or in the oven after it is turned out – or in the airing cupboard. The pieces need to dry out very gently, but not to cook or they will turn colour. The skins of bananas turn black and curl beautifully; while green or red peppers shrivel slightly to give an interesting texture. I have used avocado, too. All these add interest and an unusual quality and colour to a swag. If the skins become, by an unlucky chance, too dry and curled, do not despair and do not discard them. Soak the skin in water for a short time, pat it into the required shape, and re-dry.

Storage

Storage of the finished material is important and needs some care. Long boxes from the florist are ideal and are usually easy to obtain. Sort the material into groups – for instance, flat leaves and foliage together; cones by themselves. It is important not to allow brittle stems or prickly seedheads to fall foul of the more delicate material; a layer of paper between each group in the box will help to prevent this. I put separate leaves between the pages of a magazine, and – if they are very delicate – a face tissue between each one. Kitchen paper towels are not suitable because the surface serration imprints itself on the leaf. Put the magazine at the bottom of a box and store more material on top.

Large polythene bags are useful, but make sure there are plenty of air-holes and that they are stored in a dark place. Label the bags and the boxes and put a few crystals of silica gel in each box to counteract any damp. Gourds may be pricked to speed up the drying process, and then painted with artist's clear varnish, especially over the prick holes. The life of berries may be extended, though not indefinitely, by painting with this or by covering them with colourless nail varnish.

All the packed material must be stored in a completely damp-proof place or it will get mildew and rot away. It is also worth remembering the hungry field mice; they will track down any available seedheads and strip them bare. I well remember packing, rather hurriedly, an extra box of dried material to supplement a demonstration. When I opened the box, to my consternation, it was full of long bare stalks of corn, hollow gourds, and the spiky remains of a corn dolly. Only the mouse was missing.

Pot-pourri

There are several schools of thought about the material used for making pot-pourri, but the basis of most kinds is the rose.

Any plant material must be picked when very dry, and a rose not fully open will keep its colour better than a full-blown flower. It should be gathered in the morning, when quite dry from rain or dew; taken gently apart, care being taken not to bruise the petals; and spread out to dry for some days. Other flowers add different perfumes – lavender, scented *Geranium,* stocks, rosemary, thyme, lemon *Verbena*, jasmine, violets, and pinks (*Dianthus*). A sprig of mint or a few pieces of crushed orange or lemon peel may be added, well dried. The final perfume is really a very individual thing and can be varied according to taste. All these may be gathered when available, dried and kept aside in a warm place until the collection is complete and there is time to make the pot-pourri. Stir them occasionally and turn the large petals.

To make a pot-pourri

Put everything into a large bowl and mix thoroughly. Add an equal quantity of powdered orris root and common salt. Or there is a proprietary mixture which can be bought from most garden shops. A teacupful of rose petals, one of stocks and one of lavender would need about a tablespoon of salt and orris root. Sometimes spices are added, but this again must be left to personal taste. I prefer mine with nothing but the flower perfume – but it is fun to experiment.

Liquids can be added in very small quantities – oil of Bergamont, essence of lemon, etc ($14 \cdot 15$ grams [$\frac{1}{2}$ oz]), and the whole mass pressed down in a jar, after mixing well.

The oil will be soaked up by the petals and it can then be topped up with a sprinkle of brandy. If the mixture seems too wet, it can be dried with more salt; or, if too dry, more powdered orris. It must be kept tightly covered while this process is going on, and can then be packed into small containers. Glass jars with lids are suitable because the mixture can be seen and the lid removed and replaced at will. Take it off during the day to scent a room and replace it at night to prevent the mixture drying out. These little jars make delightful gifts if decorated with ribbon. Children can make small sachets or envelopes from any piece of thin fabric which can be filled with the mixture and put in a drawer or cupboard. I once made some of these to attach to the back of my pressed flower pictures so that they had the added attraction of perfume.

Dried flower pictures

These are different from pressed flower pictures in that no glass is used in the frame, and the plant material is all dried or preserved.

Helichrysums or any of the everlastings are very suitable for this type of work, as colour is important in its success. Cones and seedheads can be used, too, as no pressure is necessary; and several types of frame will look good. The picture can be recessed into a box frame – which is simply what it says: a shallow box built onto the back of a frame.

The design should be prepared prior to starting work and can be fixed with glue or thin wire – or even one of the new plastic clay substances. Fabric is better as a backing than paper, and a rough-textured one such as hessian, tweed or velvet is better still.

Suppliers

Certo, oil of Bergamont, glycerine, silica gel, powdered borax and orris root
from most chemists and drug stores

Araldite, Copydex, Dylon dyes, wire mesh and linseed oil
from hardware stores

Oasis, Prestige, Styrofoam also skeletonised Magnolia leaves
from most florists

Waxed paper, polythene bags
from stationers and department stores

Imported material
Natural Fern Display Limited
73 Monmouth Street, London WC2, and many florists

Aerosol cans of paint, tubes of glitter, Perspex
from most art stores

Presses
Habitat Designs Limited
77 Fulham Road, London SW3, and branches

Preserving powder
Lasting Flower, Beauchamp Marketing Limited
152a Brompton Road, London SW3